Dreaming of Dinosaurs

Poems by
John Rice

Illustrated by
Charles Fuge

MACMILLAN CHILDREN'S BOOKS

For
The Maylam family:
Esther, Esmé, Tom,
Heather and Martin

First published 1992 by
PAN MACMILLAN CHILDREN'S BOOKS
A division of Pan Macmillan Limited
Cavaye Place London SW10 9PG
and Basingstoke
Associated companies throughout the world

Reprinted 1993

ISBN 0–333–56588–6

Printed in Hong Kong

BIG, BIZARRE AND BEAUTIFUL

Millions of years before humans appeared on earth, dinosaurs roamed this planet. They lived for about 160 million years and during that vast length of time they became perfectly adapted to their environment – so much so, in fact, that they dominated the land, sea and air.

Around 65 million years ago, the dinosaurs – as well as other creatures and plants – became extinct. No one knows exactly why or how this happened; and although there are many theories, it is hard to understand why these "ruling reptiles" disappeared leaving no survivors. It is this mystery, this enigma, that continues to capture the imagination of both children and adults.

During the early part of the nineteenth century, the first fossil reptiles were found and named: these included Megalosaurus and Iguanodon. In 1841 the British scientist Richard Owen invented the name "Dinosauria" for these ancient animals. (The word comes from the Greek meaning "terrible lizard" or "fearfully great reptile".) Since those early discoveries about 340 different species of dinosaur have been identified from fossils found all over the world.

From these fossils we now know much about the habits of dinosaurs; we know what they ate, how they moved and where they lived. However, there are many things we still do *not* know. For example, we don't know what noises they made, or whether they were dark or brightly coloured – in some cases we don't even know their precise shape. These are the kinds of riddles Charles Fuge and I have set out to explore in this book. We know there are no definite solutions to these puzzles, but part of the fun has been to guess and speculate. So we have brought our imaginations and ideas to the poems and illustrations. Another of our intentions is to bring to life much of what we currently know about dinosaurs and to present this modern knowledge in an entertaining way.

Children today marvel at the wonder and mystery of the dinosaurs. For them these big, bizarre and beautiful beasts are the stuff of fantasy. They are huge, they are ferocious, they are scary! But happily they are extinct so they can't catch us.

So let's travel back in time – let's delve, let's discover, let's dream . . . of dinosaurs.

John Rice

Dinosaur Songs

Iz-skirp Iz-skirp Iz-skirp
I am Archaeopteryx.
The first feathered bird? Perhaps.
I swoop and dive above the
warm lagoons of early Europe
where I feed on insects on the wing.
Iz-skirp Iz-skirp Iz-skirp
hear me call, hear me chirp.

Hroom-Hroom-Hroom
I am Brachiosaurus.
Part giraffe, part elephant? Perhaps.
Our herd lives by the sandy edge
of the Sundance Sea
where we feed on the leaves
of the tall cycad tree.
Hroom-Hroom-Hroom
hear me trumpet, hear me bellow.

Groop-whark Groop-whark Groop-whark
I am Kronosaurus.
A whale-like sea giant? Perhaps.
I click and clatter sending my calls
through green sea and blue ocean.
Groop-whark Groop-whark Groop-whark
hear me signal, hear me sing.

Oversee the Undersea

In the music of water the reptiles swim free,
green deep in the deep green sea.

They surface and dive, a ballet in motion,
true blue in the blue true ocean.

Long-necked, smooth-skinned, their colours agree,
green deep in the deep green sea.

Twin paddles for guidance, tail-fin locomotion,
true blue in the blue true ocean.

Diabolical Dialogue

"Why do you carry
such a weight on your tail?"
said the sad-faced Torosaurus.
"To lash and to club
those who dare to assail,"
said the warrior Pinacosaurus.

"Why is your head
framed by a shield?"
said the rock-eyed Pinacosaurus.
"This frill is to frighten,
to make an enemy yield,"
said the hard-horned Torosaurus.

"Why are you covered
with a thick studded plate?"
said the grazing Torosaurus.
"So that no claw
can cut me and seal my fate,"
said the sentry Pinacosaurus.

"Why are there colours
about your face and your head?"
said the bull-voiced Pinacosaurus.
"My colours are warnings,
black, yellow and red,"
said the drumming Torosaurus.

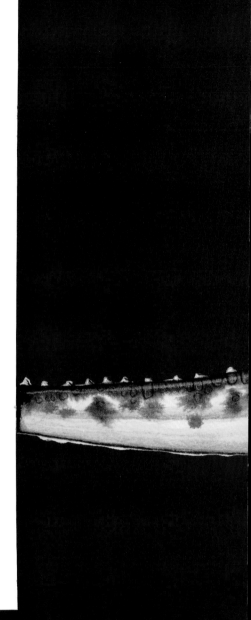

Fire Tooth

How can we suppose
you had rather large toes?

How can we surmise
your height and your size?

How can we tell
if you gave off a smell?

>Were you large as a barge?
>>tall as a wall?
>>loud as a crowd?
>>mild as a child?

How can we sense
what you did for defence?

How can we know
if you walked fast or slow?

How can we guess
what you weighed, more or less?

>Were you large as a barge?
>>tall as a wall?
>>loud as a crowd?
>>*wild* as a child?

Note: Like Barapasaurus Tagorsi (see 'The Dinosaur Who
Lost His Head', page 25) we do not know exactly what
Vulcanodon looked like as not all of its bones have
been found . . . yet.

Tyrannosaurus – Storm Fighter

Purple sky, red clouds, white lightning.
The fierce storm rages night and day.
Tyrannosaurus roars his terrible anger
and claws at the lashing rain.

Orange lava flows, yellow rivers swell.

Under his great weight
the soft earth rips apart
like a piece of cake.
The land shakes with the terrors
of fresh earthquakes.

Green hide, white teeth, blue eyed
Tyrannosaurus Rex, a killer king.

Hocus Pocus Diplodocus

Shout "top of the day" to Mr Diplodocus
whose head is so high it's out of focus!

His round body rocks, his round body rolls,
the mountains shake when he stomps and strolls.

He stands up straight on his anchor bones
and spends all day eating high pine cones.

With a neck that can bend to graze the ground
he patrols the plain without making a sound.

He has peg-shaped teeth in his halfling's head
and if he sleeps at all, it's in a bulging bed!

Dinosorry

A chubby little dinosaur,
    round and oddly bounceable:
I'd like to introduce him
    but he's sadly unannounceable.

He's tense and often edgy,
    his temper very flounceable:
he never gets to meet new friends
    for his name is UNPRONOUNCEABLE!!!

Limerickosaurus

In the days of the young dinosaurs,
the babies had sharp teeth and claws.
    Some were quite sweet,
    but others ate meat
and would grind up your toes in their jaws!

Spinosaurus Under Sail

Dawn on the desert.
Spinosaurus soaks up the yellow sun
with a sail that flutters and flaps
like a flimsy Japanese fan.

At the height of the day's heat,
she turns to face the mountain breeze:
her ribbed sail beats
like a butterfly's beautiful wings.

Dusk in the desert.
The herd of Spinosaurus settles for sleep:
their backs as bright
as a fleet of racing yachts full sail
on a shimmering sea of sand.

Good Mother Lizard

The evening light is as bright as glass
at the edge of the hissing forest.
A caring parent is Maiasaura
nuzzling her young in their muddy nest.

She stirs at the slightest sound,
slowly raising a head that's as colourful
as a painted fairground horse.

Little duckbill dinosaurs
hatched from eggs that are
as dark and dusty as picked potatoes,
they hobble-wobble around the nest
shrieking like mad violins.

But the forest speaks of danger too:
the baying of night hunters
echoes through the tall trees.

Maiasaura, Good Mother Lizard,
gathers her young around her.
She lifts her hobby-horse head and
drones her sad call at the star-sprung sky.

The plate of moon hides behind black branches.

Velociraptor, Smart Adaptor

Half a human's height,
her body lithe and light,
– *Velociraptor, smart adaptor.*

Sprinting over hot sand,
sharpened claws for a hand,
– *Velociraptor, smart adaptor.*

They follow telling tracks,
hunting prey in packs,
– *Velociraptor, smart adaptor.*

Stalking day and dark,
her call a puppy's bark,
– *Velociraptor, smart adaptor.*

Fearless, fast and fierce,
her talons slash and pierce,
– *Velociraptor, smart adaptor.*

Saltopus Skips

Saltopus skips from stone to stone,
   her camouflaged skin hides muscle and bone.
Her teeth are serrated, her sharp eyes shine,
   her yelp is a ghostly midnight whine.

Tall as a baby learning to walk
   quick as a gymnast over the rock;
Saltopus claims her innocent prey,
   hunting by night – avoiding the day.

A tail for balance, muscular jaws,
   Saltopus flexes sharpened claws.
She's the colour of sand, the colour of dust,
   a small dinosaur on Earth's changing crust.

Note: It is common to picture dinosaurs as huge creatures but some were very
   small. Saltopus was about as tall as a rabbit standing on its hind legs.

The Night Hunters

The hot day ends
as the sun sizzles on the horizon.

In the cooler evening air
the Sauronithoids search out
tiny mammals.

Large eyed to see in the dusk,
large brained for agile hunting,
they surprise their prey
with swift, sure actions.

Evening falls into night
and still the hunt goes on.
The air is filled with the cries
of victims and hunters.

The sky is scattered with stars,
the moon-sword slices the night in two,
white bones litter the sand.

Time for Dinosaurs

Digging in the desert
we found there before us
the parched white bones
of a *Longneckosaurus!*

Marching in the mountains
we heard the eerie chorus
of a long-gone herd
of *Longtailosaurus!*

Searching in the shallows
for creatures herbivorous
we stepped on the toes
of a *Longlegosaurus!*

Hunting in the hills
where the rocks ignore us
we carved out the letters
of a *Longnameosaurus . . .*

Warm Air Glider

It is the middle of a dry day.

A tailless shadow flickers over the red rocks.
Quetzalcoatlus is airborne, flying soundlessly.

She glides, soars and slides
through cushions of warm air
like a small airplane.
Her huge eyes search for carrion.
Quetzalcoatlus is airborne, flying soundlessly.

A wing-flap turn signals her descent.
The fur on her body quivers in the rush of air.
She makes an ungainly landing
on the raw, parched earth.

Kyreek-kyreek-kyreek.

Quetzalcoatlus shrieks her almost music.

Note: Quetzalcoatlus is named after an Aztec god and means
"Feathered Serpent".

Dragons of the Air

From high on the hot mountain
a preying pack of pterosaurs descends.

Sky raiders
Wing Finger, Bird Arm, Bat Glider,
Serpent Head, Tusk Jaw,
dragons of the air.

They fall

    flow

      sway, circle

        lift

   and

      float

  fall
  fall
fall . . . to land.

Wing Finger is first to touch down.
His veined wings beat like hand-drums.
His bony beak pecks at the Triceratops' hide.

After him the others land
in a clash of thin wings,
a squawk and a croak of complaints.

The raiders feed until
the red sun dips into the sea.
Then, in a storm of whipped dust,
they flap and climb awkwardly
into the depths of the darkening sky
like children's kites shrinking into black specks.

hover

fall

Dreaming of Dinosaurs

A sleepless black in the darkest night,
no movement, sound or crack of light:
time stands still, time makes a pause,
– I'm dreaming, I'm dreaming of dinosaurs.

They're posting their letters,
building a house.
They're fixing the phones
and dancing to Strauss.

They're counting their money,
swimming in pools.
They're farming the fields
and teaching in schools.

They're reading their books,
tracking the stars.
They're flying the flags
and playing guitars.

A sleepless dark in the blackest night,
no movement, sound or crack of light:
a fantasy flight that dives and soars,
– I'm dreaming, I'm dreaming of dinosaurs.

The Dinosaur Who Lost His Head
(Barapasaurus Tagorsi)

We know that your body was solid and strong,
but when it comes to your head we may have it wrong.
> We have discovered your bones
> but your skull shape's a mystery
> so your noggin's a puzzle in dinosaur history!

We know that your neck reached towering heights
and that you slept like a babe in the Jurassic nights.
> We know what you ate
> from what we've found in your gizzard
> but what was your head like you Big Legged Lizard!

Note: Barapasaurus Tagorsi (Big Legged Lizard) was a plant eater and many
of its bones have been found. However, no one has ever discovered its skull.

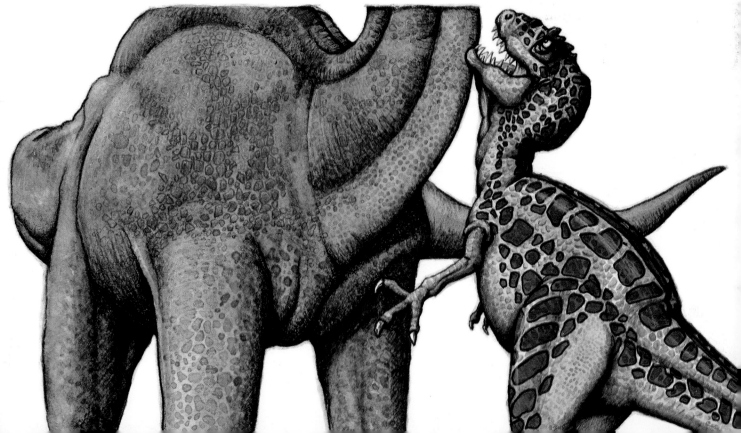

Rhyme-osaur

Out of a deep, dark mine-osaur
at roughly half past nine-osaur,
there came a sleepy stegosaur
into the warm sunshine-osaur.
He warmed his chilly spine-osaur
which made him feel divine-osaur.

He nibbled on a pine-osaur
and drank a glass of wine-osaur.
But then he saw a sign-osaur
which made him yelp and whine-osaur.
It forecast his decline-osaur –
his time had come to die-nosaur!

Claws

With my hook-like claws
I stuff my jaws
   with fish snatched from the swamp.
I wade in the mud
which cools my blood
   then I champ and chew and chomp.

I boast a crocodile crest
and a scaly pink chest,
   when fishing I'm a skilful winner.
I have a very long snout
which I poke about
   round the insides of my dinner!

I have very sharp teeth
a flat neck underneath,
   I'm a slow-moving watcher and stalker.
I'm never in a hurry
and I lived in Surrey
   and I was found by Mr Walker.

Note: Baryonx Walkeri was found in a clay-pit in Surrey,
England, by William Walker, an amateur fossil
collector, in 1983. It has been named after him but
has also earned the nickname "Claws" because of its
huge claw-bone which Mr Walker first spotted
sticking out of the clay. The discovery of this 124-
million-year-old dinosaur has proved to be the most
important find in Europe in the twentieth century.

Triceratops in Time

The moon, sharp as a blade,
slices the deep blue sky.
A sheet of shimmering coloured light
and a shaft of whiteness
announce the start of the aurora.

On a cold mountain slope,
a lone Triceratops
lifts her heavy horned head
to this wondrous theatre of light.

A moonbeam glints in her eye:
the Triceratops, in time,
shows her beauty to the sky and land.

In the valley below, a slow river
casts pale reflections
upon a herd of wandering beasts.

Look up! A comet flashes past.
Another wanderer who'll return again
when Triceratops is no more,
and again
when the river is no more
and again
when the mountain is no more
and again
when we are no more.

Steg of the Hump

Steg of the Hump is a turreted castle
with legs like thick towers
and eyes as dark as dungeons.
His bony back-plates quiver in the wind
like colourful castle flags.
His tail-spikes are the sharpest spears,
his hide a dented shield.

Steg of the Hump is a great house
with its own central heating
and its own air-conditioning.
He's bricks and cement, stone and slates.
A roofed reptile who plods timelessly
through the canyons of North America
searching for his true time, his certain self.

Downfall of the Dinosaurs

High, high in the evening sky, a pterosaur,
winged reptile, patrols the air.

Under her broad, brown wings
her silent shadow falls on the land
and waters of her timeless world:

She overflies

> the pastel shades of lagoon and plateau
> where great green beasts wade and wander:

> the soft khaki of sandflats and basins
> where trampling herds kick up duststorms:

> the red mountains, the bleached seacliffs,
> where warm air gliders swoop and soar.

The sun's spray of golden warmth ends
as the coldsoft light of moon appears.

High, high in the night-time sky
a Death Star heads for planet Earth.